Flow Spin Grow: Looking for Patterns in Nature

For Abe and Isaac—P.B.

For Henry—T.S.

Text © 2018 Patchen Barss
Illustrations © 2018 Todd Stewart

Owlkids Books acknowledges the financial support of the Canada Council for the Arts, the Ontario Arts Council, the Government of Canada through the Canada Book Fund (CBF) and the Government of Ontario through the Ontario Media Development Corporation's Book Initiative for our publishing activities.

Published in Canada by
Owlkids Books Inc.
10 Lower Spadina Avenue
Toronto, ON M5V 2Z2

Published in the United States by
Owlkids Books Inc.
1700 Fourth Street
Berkeley, CA 94710

Library and Archives Canada Cataloguing in Publication

Barss, Patchen, author
    Flow, spin, grow : looking for patterns in nature / written by Patchen Barss ; illustrations by Todd Stewart.
ISBN 978-1-77147-287-6 (hardcover)

    1. Pattern formation (Physical sciences)--Juvenile literature.
2. Pattern formation (Biology)--Juvenile literature. 3. Pattern perception--Juvenile literature. 4. Geometry in nature--Juvenile literature. 5. Mathematics in nature--Juvenile literature.
I. Stewart, Todd, 1972-, illustrator II. Title.

Q172.5.C45B37 2018   j500.201'185   C2018-900516-5

Library of Congress Control Number: 2018930806

The artwork in this book was made using a combination of silkscreen printing and digital media.

Edited by: Karen Li
Designed by: Karen Powers

Page 32 photos all Dreamstime.com: Giraffe skin texture © Anna Jurkovska; Pine bark texture © Nshirokova; Soil floor cracked pattern © Atsanee Jumee

Manufactured in Shenzhen, Guangdong, China, in March 2018, by WKT Co. Ltd.

Job #17CB2756

A   B   C   D   E   F

ONTARIO ARTS COUNCIL
CONSEIL DES ARTS DE L'ONTARIO
an Ontario government agency
un organisme du gouvernement de l'Ontario

Canada Council
for the Arts
Conseil des Arts
du Canada

Canadä

Publisher of Chirp, chickaDEE and OWL
www.owlkidsbooks.com

Owlkids Books is a division of Bayard
CANADA

Flow
Spin
Grow

Looking for Patterns in Nature

Written by **Patchen Barss**

Illustrated by **Todd Stewart**

Owlkids Books

Look, climb, dig, flow. Breathe in deep, around you go.

Twirl, whirl, swirl, grow. Explore, find more, join the show.

Look

You can find patterns almost anywhere.

Climb

A tree trunk splits.

Limbs divide.

Branches split

and split again.

Dig

Under the ground, tree roots also fork and spread. Tiny rootlets seek water and nutrients, just as leafy branches reach for sunlight.

Flow

Mountain rain and melting ice form tiny rivulets. Water burbles. Tumbling streams combine to form huge rivers. These winding, watery paths look so much like a spreading tree that we call them branches, too.

Breathe in deep

Branches also spread through your body.
They move air in and out of your lungs,
and carry blood to and from your heart.
Wherever there's flow, there's branching.

Nature loves to spin.

A tree feels solid. But it's really made up of spinning particles so small you can't even see them. They have names like protons, photons, neutrons, and electrons.

Everything you can see or touch is made out of those same tiny particles. Stones, stars, cars, people: every tiny part of them is spinning, even when they seem perfectly still.

Around you go

Twirl

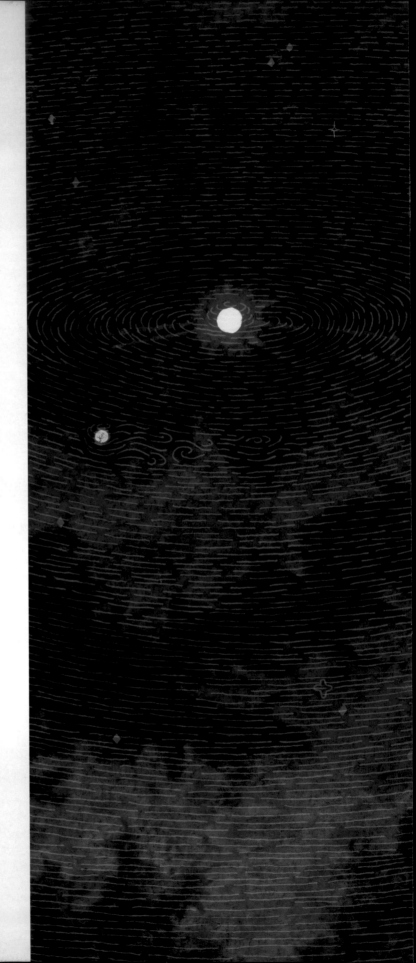

The Earth spins, too—turning
us toward the Sun and away
again, making day and night.
The Earth's gravity swings the
Moon in huge circles around
our spinning planet. The Earth
and Moon circle the Sun.

Whirl

Our whirling Sun follows an
even bigger curve around
the center of our galaxy.
Galaxies spin, too.
When moving objects push
and pull one another, they
start spinning.

Swirl

Trees and galaxies share another
pattern: they both have spirals.
You can find spirals in pine cones
and pigs' tails. In storm clouds,
swirling eddies, and seashells.
In galactic halos and inside your
own ears.

Grow

Spirals appear where things grow or shrink.

Plants and shells spiral out.

Storms and galaxies spiral in.

Explore

Patterns appear again and again, sometimes in
the most unexpected places. Try to find out why.
There's almost always an amazing explanation.
Branches tell you that something is flowing.
Moving objects make each other spin.
Spirals mean that something is growing or shrinking.

These patterns are just the start.
Keep looking. Leopard spots and ladybug
dots. Ocean waves and mountain peaks.
Lightning bolts and cracks in the sidewalk.

Find more

Patterns are everywhere you look … even in the mirror.

The same patterns that connect trees to rivers and particles to planets also connect you to all of those things.

Join the show

LOOK. DIG. EXPLORE.

You're not just discovering patterns
—you're part of the show.

Author's Note

There's a secret code hidden in the shape of things...

Pay close attention to the patterns you see, and you can discover amazing things about how the world works. If you've read this book, you know that branches are a clue that something is flowing, and spirals form when something is growing. There's so much more for you to discover, though.

Patterns can repeat in the most unexpected places. Why do a giraffe, some pine bark, and a cracked desert floor all have such similar shapes? What could an animal, a tree, and some dirt possibly have in common?

People all around the world have asked these kinds of questions for thousands of years. Artists, philosophers, and engineers all find meaning in nature's patterns, each in their own way. Farmers study the patterns of the seasons, and sailors find their way by the patterns of the stars. I love patterns because they hold such marvelous secrets about science. They tell us about hidden forces that shape our world. They connect the tiniest objects to the largest structures in the universe. They connect living things to inert rocks and soil.

The thing I find most amazing is that the forces that shaped giraffes and deserts, snails and galaxies, trees and rivers, also shaped human beings. Patterns help us understand our place in the universe.

Be watchful. Be thoughtful. Ask questions. Make connections. When you see a pattern in an unexpected place, try to find an explanation. You never know where patterns will lead you.

Want to know more about patterns?

Flow Spin Grow: Looking for Patterns in Nature is meant to inspire readers to notice how patterns shape the natural world. If you would like to learn more about specific patterns, I recommend the work of children's book author Sarah C. Campbell. She introduces fractals in *Mysterious Patterns: Finding Fractals in Nature* and explores the beautiful and compelling Fibonacci series in *Growing Patterns: Fibonacci Numbers in Nature*.

For older readers, I also recommend the works of British science journalist Philip Ball, including his book for adults, *Patterns in Nature: Why the Natural World Looks the Way It Does*.